GREAT WORDS FOR GREAT LIVING

Olutosin O. Ogunkolade

AuthorHouse™ UK Ltd.
500 Avebury Boulevard
Central Milton Keynes, MK9 2BE
www.authorhouse.co.uk
Phone: 08001974150

First published by AuthorHouse 6/22/2011

ISBN: 978-1-4567-8037-1 (sc)
ISBN: 978-1-4567-8038-8 (e)

Acknowledgements

My parents, for all the sacrifice and all you have done to
bring me this far.
All my brothers and sisters out there who truly want the best
for me and uphold me in prayers, indeed I am grateful and
appreciate your labour of love.

Dedication

This book is dedicated to all the great individuals who are either alive or passed on, they have influenced the way I see the world, the way I think, and they have contributed their own positive quota, and are still contributing it to the development of humanity. Most of the people quoted in this book are the ones I speak of.

Introduction

It suffices to say that words are very important. Positive words are like light bringing illumination in darkness and showing us which way to go, ideas emerge out of the words of people and the words of men have made men and broken men. The quotes found in this book cover different areas of life and I have taken the time to compile the ones I perceive to be informative and have a lot of meaning. I believe there is no other book out there quiet like this book in terms of the different major areas of life it touches and the diversity of individuals from different backgrounds quoted in the book, what all these individuals have in common is that they have influenced minds.

We won't get anywhere if we don't use the information and knowledge of others especially those who have gone ahead of us.

It is my hope that this book will be a useful resource in providing words that are encouraging , motivating, inspiring and maybe in some way it will bring insight and direction to the reader in areas of life where the reader needs it .

Contents

OLUTOSIN OGUNKOLADE

OLUTOSIN (DREAMS)

Each time I think of someone who has a dream Martin Luther King Jnr easily comes to mind, his dream has outlived him. Barack Obama has a dream, his dream is unfolding. Christopher Columbus had a dream, it emerged. Bishop David Oyedepo has a dream, his dreams are manifesting. James Dyson has a dream, they are manifesting through inventions.

There are certain discoveries I have made about a dream. Having a dream is not the same thing as having a fantasy, dreams in the context I refer to is having a mental picture, a vision, a clear imagination ingrained within your soul of what you want to be, do or have. It should be big enough to inspire and achievable, to motivate you.

A dream is a vision, a vision is a dream. Your dream/vision is your future.

Dreams help to keep you on track, when you don't have a dream, you miss the mark.

- -Dreams are a vital ingredient for progress.
- -Dreams don't die but the dreamer may die.
- - Dreams that are authentic outlive the dreamer.
- -Dreams come by inspiration and observation.
- -Dreams are where all achievements start.
- -Dreams give us a motivation for living.
- -Dreams are the beginning of possibilities.
- -Dreams need focus and consistency to manifest.

OLUTOSIN (FRIENDSHIP)

I wonder what life would be like without friendships, it will be lonely, boring, dry and slow. Yes slow, because friends help us achieve and they influence us positively, this give us speed in the right direction. Your friends can determine your momentum in life because our friends can be likened to the brains and hands you have which are in another body. Good friends use what they have to help us.

-Friends are necessary for successful networking.
-Friends can come in all shapes, form and complexion. We should be gender blind when it comes to friendships
-Friends are in your life for the purpose of helping you get to where you are going.
-Friends make the journey of life worthwhile.
-Friends are the "wine" of life.

OLUTOSIN (OPPORTUNITIES)

Life is full of opportunities, opportunities are part of what makes life interesting. Someone rightly said life is in phases. With every phase of life comes opportunities, as we make the most of the opportunities life presents to us at each phase, the door to the next phase of our life is opened unto us. For us to be all we can be we have to make the most of all the opportunities life presents to us.

- Opportunities sometimes will come disguised as challenges.
- Opportunities, when you use them will take you to the next level.
- Opportunities usually come disguised as hard work
- Opportunities will surely come , but it's not every chance that looks like an opportunity that has to be embraced.
- Opportunities are hidden in moments.

OLUTOSIN (MONEY)

Money can control an individual. When this happens it's a great tragedy. Man was not created for money but money was created for man, man should not be under the 'influence' of money but money should be under the influence and control of man.

The true character of most men is revealed when issues that have to do with money occur. Personally, i have seen men who were humble and well behaved change for the worse when money showed up in their lives. When a man comes under the influence of money he becomes someone else for the worse.

Money has many uses, and is very beneficial for our survival here on earth. Infact the good Book informs us that "money answers all things". Perhaps this importance of money here in our earthly journey and pursuits is what makes many people 'glorify' money beyond the ordinary. Isn't money merely printed paper recognised as a means of exchange?

There are those who worship money. When money takes the place of God in a man's heart it's called mammon.

Money is energy in tangible form that's used to manifest our dreams and desires. Money is good when you use it for noble causes but can be evil when the thoughts and desires of an individual is evil, money is not evil in itself but it takes on the character of the person in possession of it. Money is a neutral servant that obeys the wishes of its master to the latter.

Money shows up when favour is upon a life.
- Money is a lady, she is sensitive, she goes with the man who has respect for her.
- Money is a servant who shows up when you have an errand (vision) for her. No vision, no money.
- Money is preceeded by service.
- Money is the lifeline of business.
- Money is meant to be used, enjoyed and circulated.
- Money and success is geographical. There is somewhere you should be and something you should be doing.
- Money is an effect, it must be used to effect positive change.
- Money is to be used, while people are to be loved.
- Money is for manifesting your dreams. Money is part of mans creative power.
- Money flows in the direction of an idea whose time has come.
- Money gravitates in the direction of those who solve problems for others.

OLUTOSIN (SUCCESS)

Success is fine, attractive and compelling.

Perhaps that's the reason everyone wants to succeed, it's a known fact that every right thinking person wants to succeed in life and at what they do. There is a desire within us to make it and i believe it's a positive, healthy and godly desire that the Lord put within us.

For me, true success is having God's divine presence with you in all you do. Success is not merely material acquisition (though there is nothing wrong with this), success is not merely getting the best formal education, going to Ivy league schools, degrees and certificates (these things are not bad in themselves) but what profit are these things if there is no deeper meaning and understanding to life beyond what we can touch and see.

God is a suceess (don't you think so?) Afterall, He created the universe and all we see and don't see. Man is still researching and looking into what God created and will continue to do so. Our God is soo vast! And we are created in His image, thats what the Book tells us. We are created in the image of true success.

Success means many things to different people at different stages of life.

True success is our birthright, that's the truth! At whatever stage of life you are , you can succeed.

- Success has to start somewhere, so success is geographical.
- Success comes to those who help others succeed.
- Success has in the path to it, lots of distractions, bumps, and diversions
- Success has endurance as one of its building blocks.
- Success is diametrically opposed to complacency.
- Success shines through creativity and originality.
- Success is a reflection of your perspective.
- Success has a price tag attached to it. Pay it!
- Success is the reflection of what you have done with your time and gifts.
- Success visits the man who has the courage to show up for battle even if he doesn't know how he will win.
- Success is when a man finds his path and walks in it.
- Success comes when you keep your eyes on the goal.
- Success is one decision away from failure. You can't give up now.
- Success is a language, speak it!
- Success must not be left up to chance.
- Success has a very attractive and compelling nature.
- Success is the child of diligence and discipline.
- Success is preceded by understanding
- Success is a spirit.
- Success is a choice.
- Success is an attitude.
- Success is a mind game
- Success answers to consistency.

OLUTOSIN (INTEGRITY)

Integrity is that major quality found in men of worth that gives us hope that humanity still has hope. Integrity attracts favour, complements leadership, inspires belief, and gives value to all other qualities that an individual may have.

- INTEGRITY IS AS IMPORTANT AS MONEY, BUT IT'S MORE VALUABLE THAN MONEY BECAUSE IT CAN BE PACKAGED AND SOLD.
- INTEGRITY IS WHEN YOU ARE AN UPRIGHT PERSON AND YOU HAVE A GOOD NAME.
- THERE ARE DOORS INTEGRITY CAN OPEN THAT MONEY CAN'T.

OLUTOSIN (TECHNOLOGY)

Modern technology is more of a blessging to humanity than it is a vice. Technology in itself is good but its use is what determines what you get out of it. The major advantage our generation has above previous generations is in the discovery and development of technological products that have made life more comfortable and work more efficient.

- TECHNOLOGY IS AN ENDOWMENT GIVEN TO MAN TO MAKE HIM MAINTAIN HIS DOMINION, FOR THERE IS NO DOMINION WITHOUT THE EFFICIENT USE OF TIME , THIS BRINGS PRODUCTIVITY, MODERN TECHNOLOGY HAS THE POTENTIAL AND HELPS US RE-ORGANISE TIME AND SPACE.

- MODERN TECHNOLOGY CAN BE USED AND SHOULD BE USED AS AN AGENT OF CHANGE. THIS IS IT'S PROPER USE.

- WITH MODERN TECHNOLOGY COMES SOLUTIONS, BUT UNFORTUNATELY NEW CHALLENGES AND VICES TOO. THE HUMAN MIND RISES WITH TIME ABOVE SOLUTIONS OF TECHNOLOGY.

OLUTOSIN (LEADERSHIP)

Nations of the world are at a season in life where true leadership seems to be scarce and there is a huge outcry from the populace for good leadership. When there are good leaders the people rejoice, and when bad people are in positions of authority the people mourn.

The success of every enterprise, company, cooperation or nation rests and falls on its leadership. Being a leader in any capacity is not a joke.

Unfortunately we are in times where those that are perceived the most competent and qualified are failing the people. Character failure, moral decadence and lack of integrity are at an all time high. That's why i have taken some time to write on this issue.

Who is a leader? There are many definitions for leadership. It's Napoleon Bonaparte who said a leader is a dealer in hope. I agree with him. A leader is someone who has the ability to inspire hope in others for positive outcomes. You can also define a leader as someone who confers value on those within his/her sphere of influence. Leadership is all about the people you lead and less about you. A leader should be a chief servant.

- A GREAT LEADER IS A PERSON WHO STAYS AHEAD OF THE PACK BY BEING WELL INFORMED AND CONVERSANT WITH THE ISSUES AT HAND.
- A GOOD LEADER IS COMPASSIONATE AND INTOUCH WITH THE FEELINGS OF THOSE UNDER HIS SPHERE OF INFLUENCE.
- A GOOD LEADER MUST HAVE A MESSAGE THAT RESONATES WELL WITH THOSE UNDER HIS/HER SHERE OF INFLUENCE. CAPABLE LEADERS MUST HAVE SOMETHING TO SAY
- GOOD LEADERS MUST HAVE A GOOD LEVEL OF DECENCY AND INTEGRITY.
- A GREAT LEADER SHOULD BE ABLE TO MOBILISE PEOPLE AND RESOURCES FOR THE BENEFIT OF ALL.
- A GOOD AND GREAT LEADER IS A PERSON WHO HAS A HISTORY OF SERVICE. EITHER SERVICE TO AN INDIVIDUAL, SEVERAL PEOPLE OR MANY PEOPLE.
- A GOOD AND GREAT LEADER IS A PERSON WHO HAS A HISTORY OF BEING A FOLLOWER, GOOD FOLLOWERS MAKE GOOD LEADERS. THE ABILITY TO FOLLOW SHOWS HUMILITY.

OLUTOSIN (GREATNESS)

Inherent in every human being is the potential to achieve greatness. The potentials within us is enormous though it may seem small. Just like mustard seed, what we have to offer may seem insignificant but as we trade it and use it to solve problems as we journey through life, our greatness begins to emerge as our potentials blossom and mature. The qualities we manifest, the lessons we learn and apply and the right decisions we make all help to accelerate our greatness.

- GREATNESS BEGAN IN YOUR LIFE THE MOMENT YOU CHOSE TO COMMIT YOURSELF TO A WORTHWHILE GOAL OR CAUSE .

- TRUE GREATNESS BEGINS IN SOLITUDE, IT DIDNT BEGIN WHEN MEN BEGAN TO APPLAUD OR SING YOUR PRAISES. THE WORLD BEGAN TO PRAISE YOU WHEN THEY CAUGHT UP WITH YOUR GREATNESS.

- **GRASSES SPROUT FASTER THAN TREES, BUT TREES ARE SUPERIOR PLANTS TO GRASSES. DON'T ENVY THOSE WHO HAVE GONE AHEAD OF YOU.**

OLUTOSIN (LOVE)

Love is our major reason for living. Love is what keeps us alive. We live to love and we love to live. Love is the lifeline of caring for one another, the moment we stop caring in life, life becomes unworthy of living.

- IN MORE MODERN TIMES A LACK OF LOVE HAS BEEN THE BANE OF THE BLACK NATIONS THAN ANYTHING ELSE.
- LOVE IS ALL THERE REALLY IS, LOVE IS ALL THAT REALLY MATTERS.

OLUTOSIN (PURPOSE)

There is a purpose for our existence, there is a reason why we are here. The gifts and the abilities of an individual are all pointers to the assignment of that individual, the assignment of a person is what is called the purpose of that person. Your purpose is all that really matters about you. Your purpose or assignment is your reason for living.

You purpose has to be discovered, you discover it by constantly taking self – appraisals of yourself and observing and applying your talents and potential in a positive way. Your purpose cannot be separated from your ability to love your creator, yourself and your fellow man.

- LIFE IS ALL ABOUT FINDING, IT'S ALL ABOUT MAKING DISCOVERIES.
- THE PRIMARY PURPOSE OF ALL HUMAN BEINGS IS TO LOVE ONE ANOTHER, ITS IN THE PROCESS OF LOVING AND SERVING WE DISCOVER OUR GIFTS AND ABILITIES.

OLUTOSIN (HUMILITY)

Humility is that virtue and quality everyone approves of but it is hardly understood. The benefits of humility is immense and humility is a necessary requirement for getting along with other people. Humility is a winning quality, it makes other people attracted to us and makes them gravitate towards us.

- LOWLINESS IS THE PATH TO HIGLINESS, THE MAN WHO WILL SUCCEED MUST KNOW HOW TO STOOP TO CONQUER.
- A HUMBLE HEART AND A CLEAR MIND ARE VITAL REQUIREMENTS FOR ACHIEVEMENTS IN ANY FIELD OF ENDEAVOUR.

OLUTOSIN (WISDOM)

Wisdom is the ultimate of all qualities, it gives us direction, discernment, foresight, solutions and the right perception. A man with wisdom will survive, thrive and prosper. Wisdom makes our life worth living, and it gives us a sense of timing.

- BECAUSE THE MIND IS THE SEAT OF WISDOM, I'LL DEFINE WISDOM AS AN UNUSUAL SHARPNESS OF THE MIND.
- WISDOM IS BIRTHED IN THE SPIRIT OF MAN, BUT IT RESIDES IN THE MIND OF MAN AND IS EXPRESSED THROUGH THE MOUTH AND ACTIONS OF MAN.
- WISDOM DEMANDS THAT WE SPEAK LESS AND LISTEN MORE BECAUSE MANY THINGS IN THIS WORLD ARE NOT WHAT THEY SEEM.
- WITH WISDOM COMES SOME LEVEL OF DISCERNMENT. WISDOM UNDERSTANDS THAT BECAUSE A THING LOOKS GOOD DOESN'T MEAN IT'S GOOD FOR YOU.

OLUTOSIN (FAITH)

A man of faith is a man of courage, faith is that essential quality that makes us stand for something. A man of faith doesn't fall for everything but stands strong for that which he knows. Our faith cannot be separated from our convictions, belief and understanding. Faith opens us up to strength and power we never knew we had, and that we do not see. It is faith that makes the impossible possible for us.

- FAITH IS THE FORCE THAT DELIVERS OUR INHERITANCE TO US ON THE EARTH.
- FAITH HAS THE POWER TO CONTROL THE ELEMENTS AND NATURE.
- FAITH IS NOT BLIND, IT CAN SEE. FAITH HAS EYES.
- IT IS FAITH THAT TURNS ORDINARY MEN INTO SUPER-MEN.
- FAITH DOES NOT DRAW BACK.

OLUTOSIN (IMAGINATION)

Our imagination has been given to us for a reason. We are supposed to train our imaginative faculties, and use it to see. Within our imagination lies our possibilities and what we can be.

- IF NO ONE CAN STOP YOU FROM USING YOUR IMAGINATION, NOBODY CAN STOP YOU FROM SUCCEEDING.
- YOUR IMAGINATION IS YOUR ABILITY TO SEE WITH THE EYES OF YOUR MIND.
- ONE OF THE MOST UNFORTUNATE THINGS THAT HAPPENS TO ADULTS IS THAT WE LEAVE OUR ABILITY TO IMAGINE IN OUR CHILDHOOD.

OLUTOSIN (CREATIVITY)

Creativity is true success.

We become creative when we are in the place of service. It's in the multitude of work and thoughts, creative ideas come. Creativity comes to us when we are functioning with a heart to serve and a willingness to do better wherever we are.

- EVERY HUMAN BEING IS CREATIVE IN SOMEWAY BUT NOT EVERYONE USES THEIR CREATIVITY.
- YOUR SUCCESS IS IN YOUR ABILITY TO BE CREATIVE.
- THE REALM OF YOUR IMAGINATION IS YOUR CREATIVE REALM.
- CREATIVITY CAN COME ABOUT IN THE PLACE OF MEDITATION ON A PARTICULAR ISSUE.

Notes

ALBERT EINSTEIN

ALBERT EINSTEIN

- THE MAN WHO HAS LOST HIS IMAGINATION HAS LOST HIS CHANCE.
- TWO THINGS ARE INFINITE: THE UNIVERSE AND HUMAN STUPIDITY, I AM NOT SURE ABOUT THE UNIVERSE.
- GREAT MINDS HAVE ALWAYS RECEIVED VIOLENT OPPOSITION FROM MEDIOCRE MINDS
- IF a IS A SUCCESS IN LIFE, THEN a EQUALS x PLUS y PLUS z. WORK IS x; y IS PLAY; AND z IS KEEPING YOUR MOUTH SHUT
- IT'S NOT THAT I AM SO SMART; IT'S JUST THAT I STAY WITH PROBLEMS LONGER.

Notes

_____

_____

_____

_____

_____

_____

_____

_____

_____

BENJAMIN DISRAELI

- WITH WORDS WE GOVERN MEN.
- WATCH YOUR THOUGHTS, FOR THEY BECOME WORDS. WATCH YOUR WORDS, FOR THEY BECOME ACTIONS. WATCH YOUR ACTIONS FOR THEY BECOME HABITS. WATCH YOUR HABITS FOR THEY BECOME CHARACTER. WATCH YOUR CHARACTER, FOR IT BECOMES DESTINY.
- AS A GENERAL RULE THE MOST SUCCESSFUL MAN IN LIFE IS THE MAN WHO HAS THE BEST INFORMATION.
- NEVER APOLOGISE FOR SHOWING FEELING. WHEN YOU DO, YOU APOLOGISE FOR TRUTH.
- GRIEF IS THE AGONY OF AN INSTANT, THE INDULGENCE OF GRIEF THE BLUNDER OF A LIFE.

Notes

_____

_____

_____

_____

_____

_____

_____

_____

_____

_____

MOTHER TERESA

IF WE HAVE NO PEACE I THINK IT'S
BECAUSE WE HAVE FORGOTTEN THAT
WE BELONG TO EACH OTHER

Notes

_____

_____

_____

_____

_____

_____

_____

_____

_____

_____

JESSAMYN WEST

FICTION REVEALS TRUTH THAT REALITY OBSCURES.

Notes

_____

_____

_____

_____

_____

_____

_____

_____

_____

_____

JONATHAN SWIFT

FOR IN REASON, ALL GOVERNEMENT WITHOUT THE CONSENT OF THE GOVERNED IS THE VERY DEFINITION OF SLAVERY

Notes

_____

_____

_____

_____

_____

_____

_____

_____

_____

_____

TONY BLAIR

IT IS NOT AN ARROGANT GOVERNMENT
THAT CHOOSES PRIORITIES, IT'S AN
IRRESPONSIBLE GOVERNMENT THAT
FAILS TO CHOOSE.

Notes

ADLAI STEVENSON

PATRIOTISM IS NOT SHORT, FRENZIED
OUTBURSTS OF EMOTION, BUT THE
TRANQUIL AND STEADY DEDICATION OF
A LIFETIME.

Notes

THOMAS JEFFERSON

- WHEN WE WANT TO COVER OUR OWN MISTAKES, WE ALWAYS TRY TO POINT THE FINGER AT OTHERS
- ALL TYRANNY NEEDS TO GAIN A FOOTHOLD IS FOR PEOPLE OF GOOD CONSCIENCE TO REMAIN SILENT.
- A COWARD IS MUCH MORE EXPOSED TO QUARRELS THAN A MAN OF SPIRIT.
- LEAVE ALL THE AFTERNOON FOR EXERCISE AND RECREATION, WHICH ARE AS NECESSARY AS READING. I WILL RATHER SAY MORE NECESSARY BECAUSE HEALTH IS WORTH MORE THAN LEARNING.

Notes

_____

_____

_____

_____

_____

_____

_____

_____

_____

_____

ABRAHAM LINCOLN

ABRAHAM LINCOLN

- SURELY GOD WOULD NOT HAVE CREATED SUCH A BEING AS MAN TO EXIST ONLY FOR A DAY ! NO, NO, MAN WAS MADE FOR IMMORTALITY.
- YOU CANNOT ESCAPE THE RESPONSIBILITY OF TOMORROW BY EVADING IT TODAY.
- I LEAVE YOU HOPING THE LAMP OF LIBERTY WILL BURN IN YOUR BOSSOMS UNTIL THERE SHALL NO LONGER BE A DOUBT THAT ALL MEN ARE CREATED FREE AND EQUAL.
- LET US HAVE FAITH THAT RIGHT MAKES MIGHT, AND IN THAT FAITH, LET US, DARE TO DO OUR DUTY AS WE UNDERSTAND IT
- THOSE WHO DENY FREEDOM TO OTHERS , DESERVE IT NOT FOR THEMSELVES; AND UNDER A JUST GOD, CANNOT LONG RETAIN IT.
- MAKE TIME TO STUDY, THE SECRET OF THE AGES IS IN BOOKS.

- IF YOU ONCE FORFEIT THE CONFIDENCE OF YOUR FELLOW CITIZENS, YOU CAN NEVER REGAIN THEIR RESPECT AND SELF- ESTEEM. IT IS TRUE YOU MAY FOOL ALL THE PEOPLE SOME OF THE TIME; YOU CAN EVEN FOOL SOME OF THE PEOPLE SOME OF THE TIME; BUT YOU CAN'T FOOL ALL THE PEOPLE ALL OF THE TIME.

Notes

_____

_____

_____

_____

_____

_____

_____

_____

_____

_____

RON PAUL

ALL INITIATION OF FORCE IS A VIOLATION OF SOMEONE ELSE'S RIGHTS, WHETHER INITIATED BY AN INDIVIDUAL OR THE STATE, FOR THE BENEFIT OF AN INDIVIDUAL OR GROUP OF INDIVIDUALS EVEN IF IT'S SUPPOSED TO BE FOR THE BENEFIT OF ANOTHER INDIVIDUAL OR GROUP OF INDIVIDUALS

Notes

_____

_____

_____

_____

_____

_____

_____

_____

_____

_____

_____

JIMMY CARTER

- I SAY TO YOU QUIET FRANKLY THAT THE TIME FOR RACIAL DISCRIMINATION IS OVER.
- AGGRESSION UNOPPOSED BECOMES A CONTAGIOUS DISEASE.

Notes

_____

_____

_____

_____

_____

_____

_____

_____

_____

_____

ROWAN WILLIAMS
(Archbishop of Canterbury)

THE ROAD OF TRUE RACIAL JUSTICE AS
PROVED AS WE ALWAYS KNEW IT WOULD, A
LONG AND ARDUOUS DISTANCE WE HAVE
TRAVELLED...GREAT   ACHIEVEMENTS
COME WITH LONGEVITY

Notes

JOHN WILLIAM LUBBOCK
(banker, astronomer and mathematician)

A WISE SYSTEM OF EDUCATION WILL AT
LAST TEACH US HOW LITTLE MAN YET
KNOWS, HOW MUCH HE HAS STILL TO
LEARN.

Notes

ARCHBISHOP DESMOND TUTU

- CHILDREN ARE A WONDERFUL GIFT. THEY HAVE AN EXTRAORDINARY CAPACITY TO SEE INTO THE HEART OF THINGS AND TO EXPOSE SHAM AND HUMBUG FOR WHAT THEY ARE.
- A PERSON IS A PERSON BECAUSE HE RECOGNISES OTHERS AS PERSONS.

Notes

BENJAMIN FRANKLIN
(Inventor, Journalist, stateman)

A MAN WRAPPED UP IN HIMSELF MAKES
A VERY SMALL BUNDLE.

Notes

_____

_____

_____

_____

_____

_____

_____

_____

_____

_____

MARK TWAIN

- REALLY GREAT PEOPLE MAKE YOU FEEL THAT YOU, TOO, CAN BECOME GREAT.
- CLOTHES MAKE THE MAN. NAKED PEOPLE HAVE LITTLE OR NO INFLUENCE ON SOCIETY.
- ADVERTISEMENTS CONTAIN THE ONLY TRUTH TO BE RELIED ON IN A NEWSPAPER
- THUNDER IS GOOD, THUNDER IS IMPRESSIVE, BUT IT IS THE LIGHTNING THAT DOES THE WORK.

Notes

_____

_____

_____

_____

_____

_____

_____

_____

_____

_____

CHRIS OKOTIE
(Politician, minstrel and minister)

GREATNESS DOES NOT CONSIST IN BEING
GREAT BUT IN THE ABILITY TO MAKE
OTHERS GREAT.

Notes

BO BENNETT

ENTHUSIASM IS EXCITEMENT WITH INSPIRATION, MOTIVATION AND A PINCH OF CREATIVITY.

Notes

MARY ANNE RADMACHER

COURAGE DOESN'T ALWAYS ROAR. SOMETIMES COURAGE IS THE QUIET VOICE AT THE END OF THE DAY SAYING, I WILL TRY AGAIN TOMORROW.

Notes

WINSTON CHURCHILL

- SUCCESS IS NOT FINAL, FAILURE IS NOT FATAL: IT IS THE COURAGE TO CONTINUE THAT COUNTS.
- WE MAKE A LIVING BY WHAT WE GET, BUT WE MAKE A LIFE BY WHAT WE GIVE.

Notes

_____

_____

_____

_____

_____

_____

_____

_____

_____

_____

_____

TOMMY LASORDA

THE DIFFERENCE BETWEEN THE
IMPOSSIBLE AND THE POSSIBLE LYES IN
A PERSONS DETEMINATION.

Notes

C.S LEWIS

A PROUD MAN IS ALWAYS LOOKING DOWN ON THINGS AND PEOPLE; AND OFCOURSE, AS LONG AS YOU ARE LOOKING DOWN, YOU CAN'T SEE SOMETHING THAT'S ABOVE YOU.

Notes

SIR ISAAC NEWTON

- DON'T GO AROUND SAYING THE WORLD OWES YOU A LIVING. THE WORLD OWES YOU NOTHING. IT WAS HERE FIRST.
- I HAVE NEVER LET MY SCHOOLING INTERFERE WITH MY EDUCATION.

- IF I HAVE EVER SEEN FURTHER THAN OTHERS IT'S BY STANDING ON THE SHOULDERS OF GIANTS, MEN WHO HAVE GONE BEFORE ME.
- IF I HAVE EVER MADE ANY VALUABLE DISCOVERIES , IT HAS BEEN OWING MORE TO PATIENT ATTENTION THAN TO ANY OTHER TALENT.

Notes

_____

_____

_____

_____

_____

_____

_____

_____

_____

_____

BENJAMIN NETANYAHU

WE DON'T POINT A PISTOL AT OUR OWN FOREHEAD. THIS IS NOT THE WAY TO CONDUCT NEGOTIATIONS.

Notes

_____

_____

_____

_____

_____

_____

_____

_____

_____

_____

ARIEL SHARON

A LIE SHOULD BE TRIED IN A PLACE WHERE
IT WILL ATTRACT THE ATTENTION OF
THE WORLD.

_____

_____

_____

_____

_____

_____

_____

_____

_____

_____

APHRA BEHN

EACH MOMENT OF A HAPPY LOVERS
HOUR IS WORTH AN AGE OF DULL AND
COMMON LIFE.

Notes

_____

_____

_____

_____

_____

_____

_____

_____

_____

_____

PAUL NEWMAN
(Legendary movie star)

PEOPLE STAY MARRIED BECAUSE THEY
WANT TO, NOT BECAUSE THE DOORS
ARE LOCKED.

Notes

_____

_____

_____

_____

_____

_____

_____

_____

_____

_____

DOUG LARSON

- MORE MARRIAGES MIGHT SURVIVE IF THE PARTNERS REALIZE THAT SOMETIMES THE BETTER COMES AFTER THE WORSE.
- DONT MARRY SOMEONE YOU CAN LIVE WITH, MARRY SOMEONE YOU CANNOT LIVE WITHOUT.

Notes

JIMMY EVANS

REMEMBER THAT A SUCCESSFUL MARRIAGE DEPENDS ON TWO THINGS (1) FINDING THE RIGHT PERSON (11)BEING THE RIGHT PERSON.

Notes

_____

_____

_____

_____

_____

_____

_____

_____

_____

_____

TOM KRAUSE

- COURAGE IS THE DISCOVERY THAT YOU MAY NOT WIN, TRYING WHEN YOU KNOW YOU CAN LOOSE.
- IF YOU DO WHAT YOU KNOW YOU CAN DO- YOU NEVER DO VERY MUCH.

Notes

CHARLIE TREMENDOUS JONES

THE KEY TO A SUCCESSFUL MARRIAGE
IS INTEGRITY NOT COMPATIBILITY,
COMPATIBILITY CAN BE BASED ON
DECEPTION, INTEGRITY IS FAITHFUL
AND TRUE.

Notes

_____

_____

_____

_____

_____

_____

_____

_____

_____

_____

SIR RICHARD BRANSON

I NEVER GET THE ACCOUNTANTS IN BEFORE I START UP A BUSINESS. IT'S DONE ON GUT FEELING, ESPECIALLY IF I CAN SEE THEY ARE TAKING THE MICKY OUT ON THE CUSTOMER.

Notes

_____

_____

_____

_____

_____

_____

_____

_____

_____

_____

JERRY SCRIVEN

THE SECRET OF THE WOLF IS THE PACK
AND THE SECRET OF THE PACK IS THE
WOLF.

Notes

_____

_____

_____

_____

_____

_____

_____

_____

_____

JAMES EARL JONES
(African American Actor)

- YOUR OWN NEED TO BE, SHINES OUT OF ANY DREAM OR CREATION YOU IMAGINE.
- WHEN I READ GREAT LITERATURE, GREAT DRAMA, I FEEL THE HUMAN MIND HAS NOT ACHIEVED ANYTHING GREATER THAN THE ABILITY TO SHARE FEELINGS AND THOUGHTS THROUGH LANGUAGE.

_____

_____

_____

_____

_____

_____

_____

_____

_____

_____

DEXTER YAGER
(Business and Sales Mogul)

- IF THE DREAM IS BIG ENOUGH THE FACTS DON'T MATTER .
- THE BEST REASONS FOR HAVING DREAMS IS THAT IN DREAMS NO REASONS ARE NECESSARY.

Notes

_____

_____

_____

_____

_____

_____

_____

_____

_____

_____

JAMES DYSON (Inventor)

ENJOY FAILURE AND LEARN FROM IT. YOU
CAN NEVER LEARN FROM SUCCESS.

Notes

Dr DAVID OYEDEPO
(Author, Educationist, and Minister)

- IF YOU'VE LOST ANYTHING GOD IS THE ONLY REASON YOU'VE NOT LOST EVERYTHING.
- PEOPLE WHO DO THINGS ANYHOW END UP ANYHOW YOUR PERSPECTIVE WILL DETEMINE YOUR PLACEMENT.
- YOU DON'T WALK INTO POWER, YOU FIGHT YOUR WAY INTO POWER.
- LIFE IS WARFARE NOT FUNFARE
- IT IS PATIENCE THAT WINS THE RACE OF LIFE.

Notes

_____

_____

_____

_____

_____

_____

_____

_____

_____

_____

HAILE SELASSIE 1,
(Statesman and Emperor of Ethiopia)

- GOD AND HISTORY WILL REMEMBER YOUR JUDGEMENT.
- UNTIL THE PHILOSPHY WHICH HOLDS ON A RACE AS SUPERIOR AND ANOTHER AS INFERIOR IS FINALLY AND PERMANENTLY DISCREDITED AND ABANDONED, EVERYWHERE IS WAR AND UNTIL THERE ARE NO LONGER FIRST-CLASS OR SECOND CLASS CITIZENS OF ANY NATION, UNTIL THE COLOUR OF MANS SKIN IS NO MORE SIGNIFICANT THAN THE COLOUR OF HIS EYES. AND UNTIL THE BASIC HUMAN RIGHTS ARE EQUALLY GUARANTEED TO ALL WITHOUT REGARD TO RACE, THERE IS NO WAR. AND UNTIL THAT DAY THE DREAM OF LASTING PEACE, WORLD CITIZENSHIP, RULE OF INTERNATIONAL MORALITY WILL REMAIN BUT A FLEETING ILLUSION TO BE PURSUED BUT NEVER ATTAINED...NOW EVERYWHERE IS WAR.

- THROUGHOUT HISTORY IT HAS BEEN THE INACTION OF THOSE WHO COULD HAVE ACTED, THE INDIFFERENCE OF THOSE WHO COULD HAVE KNOWN BETTER, THE SILENCE OF THE VOICE OF JUSTICE WHEN IT MATTERED MOST THAT HAS MADE IT POSSIBLE FOR EVIL TO TRIUMPH.

Notes

_____

_____

_____

_____

_____

_____

_____

_____

_____

_____

_____

MARTIN LUTHER KING JNR

- WE ALL HAVE THE DRUM MAJOR INSTINCT. WE ALL WANT TO BE IMPORTANT, TO SURPASS OTHERS, TO ACHIEVE DISTINCTION, TO LEAD THE PARADE. ...AND THE GREAT ISSUE OF LIFE IS TO HARNESS THE DRUM MAJOR INSTINCT. IT IS A GOOD INSTINCT IF YOU DON'T DISTORT IT AND PERVERT IT. DON'T GIVE IT UP. KEEP FEELING THE NEED FOR BEING IMPORTANT. KEEP FEELING THE NEED FOR BEING FIRST. BUT I WANT YOU TO BE THE FIRST IN BEING IN LOVE. I WANT YOU TO BE THE FIRST IN MORAL EXCELLENCE. I WANT YOU TO BE THE FIRST IN GENEROSITY.
- THERE COMES A TIME WHEN SILENCE IS BETRAYAL.
- UNEARNED SUFFERING CAN BE REDEEMED.
- UNLESS A MAN HAS FOUND SOMETHING HE CAN DIE FOR HE IS NOT FIT TO BE CALLED A MAN.
- FAITH IS TAKING THE FIRST STEP EVEN WHEN YOU DON'T SEE THE WHOLE STAIRCASE.

Notes

_____

_____

_____

_____

_____

_____

_____

_____

_____

_____

_____

TUNDE BAKARE
(Preacher and convener of the Save Nigeria Group)

DELEGATION WITHOUT SUPRVISION LEADS TO ABANDONMENT.

Notes

CZECH PROVERB.

DO NOT PROTECT YOURSELF BY A FENCE
BUT RATHER BY YOUR FRIENDS

MICHAEL ANGELO

I SAW THE ANGEL IN THE MARBLE AND
CARVED UNTIL I SET HIM FREE

Notes

JAPANESE PROVERB

ONE KIND WORD CAN WARM THREE WINTER MONTHS .

Notes

_____

_____

_____

_____

_____

_____

_____

_____

_____

_____

VINCENT VAN GOGH

I DREAM MY PAINTING AND THEN I
PAINT MY DREAM

Notes

13th DALAI LAMA

BE KIND WHENEVER POSSIBLE, IT IS ALWAYS POSSIBLE.

Notes

_____

_____

_____

_____

_____

_____

_____

_____

_____

_____

GUSTAVO ADOLFO BECQUER

THE SOUL THAT CAN SPEAK THROUGH
THE EYES CAN ALSO KISS WITH A GAZE.

Notes

_____

_____

_____

_____

_____

_____

_____

_____

_____

_____

LEONARDO DA VINCI

YOU CAN COPY A MANS IDEAS BUT YOU
CAN'T COPY HIS BRAINS.

Notes

_____

_____

_____

_____

_____

_____

_____

_____

_____

_____

JOEL GARFINKLE
(Career coach)

FOR A MAN TO LOCATE HIS OWN PATH
AND WALK IN IT THAT IS SUCCESS.

Notes

_____

_____

_____

_____

_____

_____

_____

_____

_____

WILLIAM BOOTH
(founder of the Salvation Army)

WORK AS IF EVERYTHING DEPENDS ON WORK AND PRAY AS IF EVERYTHING DEPENDS ON PRAYER.

Notes

_____

_____

_____

_____

_____

_____

_____

_____

_____

CHINESE PROVERB

WHEN I DIG ANOTHER OUT OF TROUBLE, THE HOLE FROM WHICH I LIFT HIM IS THE PLACE WHERE I BURY MY OWN.

Notes

_____

_____

_____

_____

_____

_____

_____

_____

_____

_____

MOHAMMED ALI

A POSITIVE SELF IMAGE IS NECESSARY, I
HAVE ALWAYS BELIEVED IT IS ORDAINED
I CANNOT LOOSE.

Notes

_____

_____

_____

_____

_____

_____

_____

_____

LES BROWN
(Author and Motivational speaker)

- THERE ARE THINGS THAT WILL HAPPEN TO YOU IN LIFE THAT ONLY PRAYER CAN CHANGE.
- YOU'VE GOT TO BE WILLING TO GIVE UP WHO YOU ARE TO BECOME WHO YOU SHOULD BE.
- IT IS YOUR DUTY TO INVENT YOUR OWN FUTURE.
- TO MAKE THINGS HAPPEN YOU'VE GOT TO KEEP ON STRIKING.
- IF YOU GO THROUGH LIFE CASUAL; YOU'LL END UP A CASUALTY.
- DONT LET PEOPLE TELL YOU WHAT YOU CAN'T DO IF THEY HAVEN'T DONE IT.
- IT IS LONELY AT THE TOP BUT YOU EAT BETTER.
- DON'T SELL OUT ON YOURSELF YOU DESERVE YOUR DREAM.

Notes

_____

_____

_____

_____

_____

_____

_____

_____

_____

_____

_____

BILL GATES

- WE USED TOOLS IN THE PAST TO LEVERAGE OUR MUSCLES. WE USE TOOLS TODAY TO LEVERAGE OUR MINDS.
- SMART COMPANIES WILL COMBINE INTERNET SERVICES AND PERSONAL CONTACT IN PROGRAMMES THAT GIVE THEIR CUSTOMERS THE BENEFIT OF BOTH KINDS OF INTERACTION.
- TIMING, SKILL, FAVOUR HAVE BEEN MAJOR FACTORS OF WHAT I'VE BEEN ABLE TO DO.

Notes

_____

_____

_____

_____

_____

_____

_____

_____

_____

SAM WALTON

TO SUCCEED, YOU HAVE TO STAY OUT
INFRONT OF THAT CHANGE.

Notes

_____

_____

_____

_____

_____

_____

_____

_____

_____

_____

SOPHIE TUCKER

I HAVE BEEN RICH AND I HAVE BEEN
POOR. RICH IS BETTER.

Notes

_____

_____

_____

_____

_____

_____

_____

_____

_____

_____

NAPOLEON HILL

ALL ACHIEVEMENT AND ALL EARTHLY
RICHES HAVE THEIR BEGINNINGS IN AN
IDEA OR DREAM.

Notes

_____

_____

_____

_____

_____

_____

_____

_____

_____

JACK WELCH
(C.EO. General Electric)

ANYTIME THERE IS CHANGE, THERE IS OPPORTUNITY. SO IT IS IMPORTANT THAT AN ORGANISATION GETS ENERGISED RATHER THAN PARALYSED.

_____

_____

_____

_____

_____

_____

_____

_____

_____

_____

GEORGE ELLIOT.

WHAT GREATER THING IS THERE THAN FOR TWO HUMAN SOULS TO FEEL THAT THEY ARE JOINED... TO STRENGTHEN EACH OTHER...TO BE ONE WITH EACH OTHER IN SILENT UNSPEAKABLE MEMORIES.

Notes

_____

_____

_____

_____

_____

_____

_____

_____

_____

MIGNON MCLAUGHLIN

IN THE ARITHMETIC OF LOVE, ONE PLUS ONE EQUALS EVERYTHING, AND TWO MINUS ONE EQUALS NOTHING.

Notes

_____

_____

_____

_____

_____

_____

_____

_____

_____

_____

OPRAH WINFREY

I DON'T BELIEVE IN FAILURE, IT'S NOT
FAILURE IF YOU ENJOYED THE PROCESS.

Notes

_____

_____

_____

_____

_____

_____

_____

_____

_____

_____

145

BILL COSBY

I DON'T KNOW THE SECRET TO SUCCESS
BUT I KNOW THE KEY TO FAILURE IS TO
TRY AND PLEASE EVERYONE.

Notes

_____

_____

_____

_____

_____

_____

_____

_____

_____

RALPH WALDO EMERSON

- LIFE IS SHORT BUT THERE IS ALWAYS ENOUGH TIME FOR COURTESY.
- THE WHOLE UNIVERSE IS AGAINST YOU IF YOU HAVE LOST CONFIDENCE IN YOURSELF.
- A HERO IS NO BRAVER THAN AN ORDINARY MAN, BUT HE IS BRAVER FIVE MINUTES LONGER
- ALL I HAVE SEEN TEACHES ME TO TRUST THE CREATOR FOR ALL I HAVE NOT SEEN
- BEWARE WHEN THE GREAT GOD LETS LOOSE A THINKER ON THIS PLANET
- CHARACTER IS HIGHER THAN INTELLECT...A GREAT SOUL WILL BE STRONG TO LIVE, AS WELL AS TO THINK
- DONT WASTE YOURSELF ON REJECTION, NOR BARK AGAINST THE BAD, BUT CHANT THE BEAUTY OF THE GOOD.
- IF A MAN WRITES A BETTER BOOK, PREACHES A BETTER SERMON OR MAKES A BETTER MOUSETRAP THAN HIS NEIGHBOUR, THE WORLD WILL MAKE A BEATEN PATH TO HIS DOOR.

- MOST PEOPLE ARE USUALLY MORE CAREFUL OF THEIR MONEY THAN THEIR PRINCIPLES.
- THE FIRST WEALTH IS HEALTH.
- EVERY CALAMITY IS A SPUR AND A VALUABLE HINT.

Notes

BILLY FLORENCE

THE BIGGER THE LEVEL OF THE
CHALLENGE, THE BIGGER THE WINNER
WILL BE.

Notes

_____

_____

_____

_____

_____

_____

_____

_____

_____

_____

MIKE MURDOCK

- ALL SUCCESS IS BUILT ON INCONVENIENCE.
- YOU WILL NEVER CHANGE YOUR LIFE UNTIL YOU CHANGE SOMETHING YOU DO DAILY.

Notes

FRED HARTEIS

FOCUS OR FIZZLE. IT'S A CHOICE.

Notes

EARL NIGHTINGALE

SUCCESS IS THE PROGRESSIVE REALISATION OF WHAT YOU HAVE TO OVERCOME.

Notes

ANDREW CARNEGIE

IMPOSSIBLE IS POTENTIAL, IT'S THE OPPORTUNITY TO PROVE SOMETHING.

Notes

MARIO ANDRETTI
(Race car driver)

IF YOU THINK YOU HAVE THINGS UNDER CONTROL, YOU'RE NOT GOING FAST ENOUGH, IT'S THE SAME THING WITH CARS AND LIFE.

Notes

_____

_____

_____

_____

_____

_____

_____

_____

_____

_____

_____

RICHARD BACH

SOME CHOICES WE LIVE NOT ONLY
ONCE BUT A THOUSAND TIMES OVER,
REMEMBERING THEM FOR THE REST OF
OUR LIVES.

Notes

_____

_____

_____

_____

_____

_____

_____

_____

_____

_____

DWIGHT D. EINSENHOWER

NEITHER A WISE MAN NOR A BRAVE MAN
LYES DOWN ON THE TRACKS OF HISTORY
TO WAIT FOR THE TRAIN OF FUTURE TO
RUN OVER HIM.

Notes

_____

_____

_____

_____

_____

_____

_____

_____

_____

_____

SWAMAI SIVANANDA

PUT YOUR HEART, MIND, INTELLECT AND SOUL EVEN TO YOUR SMALLEST ACTS. THIS IS THE SECRET OF SUCCESS.

Notes

JOHANN VON GOETHE

KNOWING IS NOT ENOUGH; WE MUST
APPLY. WILLING IS NOT ENOUGH; WE
MUST DO.

Notes

MAHATMA GHANDI

- INDOLENCE IS A DELIGHTFUL BUT
  DISTRESSING STATE, WE MUST BE
  DOING SOMETHING TO BE HAPPY.
- FREEDOM IS NOT WORTH HAVING IF
  IT DOES NOT INCLUDE THE FREEDOM
  TO MAKE MISTAKES
- ALWAYS AIM AT COMPLETE HARMONY
  OF THOUGHT AND WORD AND DEED.
  ALWAYS AIM AT PURIFYING YOUR

THOUGHTS AND EVERYTHING WILL
BE WELL.

- IT IS HEALTH THAT IS REAL WEALTH,
  NOT PIECES OF GOLD AND SILVER.

- ONE NEEDS TO BE SLOW TO FORM
  CONVICTIONS, BUT ONCE FORMED
  THEY MUST BE DEFENDED AGAINST
  THE HEAVIEST ODDS.

- THE WEAK CAN NEVER FORGIVE .
  FORGIVENESS IS THE ATTRIBUTE OF
  THE STRONG.

Notes

_____

_____

_____

_____

_____

_____

_____

_____

_____

_____

PAT WILLIAMS

- THE ONLY TALENT IS PERSISTENCE.
- NO SUCCESS SHOULD JUSTIFY A BOKEN FAMILY.
- THE DIFFERENCE BETWEEN INVOLVEMENT AND COMMITMENT CAN BE EXEMPLIFIED BY A HAM OMELETTE. THE CHICKEN GOT INVOLVED; THE PIG WAS COMMITTED.

Notes

_____

_____

_____

_____

_____

_____

_____

_____

_____

SAHA HASHIMI

LEAP ! AND THE NET WILL APPEAR.

Notes

MARK GORMAN

THE GREATEST GIFT IS TO LOOK IN THE
MIRROR AND SEE WHO YOU'VE BECOME
IN THE PROCESS OF ACHIEVING YOUR
DREAM.

Notes

FREDERICK
EIKERENKOETTER
(REV. IKE)

YOU CAN ONLY ACHIEVE WHAT YOU CAN
VISUALISE.

Notes

_____

_____

_____

_____

_____

_____

_____

_____

_____

_____

BOB GREGSON

THE BEST LEADERS ARE THE BEST
SERVERS

Notes

_____

_____

_____

_____

_____

_____

_____

_____

_____

_____

HENRY FORD

THINKING IS THE HARDEST JOB THERE
IS, THAT'S WHY FEW PEOPLE DO IT.

Notes

_____

_____

_____

_____

_____

_____

_____

_____

_____

_____

SIR EDMUND HILLARY
(the first man to climb the top Of mount Everest)

IT'S NOT THE MOUNTAINS WE CONQUER BUT CONQUERING OURSELVES THAT MATTERS.

Notes

_____

_____

_____

_____

_____

_____

_____

_____

_____

THOMAS PAINE

AN ARMY OF PRINCIPLES WILL PENETRATE
WHERE AN ARMY OF SOLDIERS WILL
NOT...AND IT WILL CONQUER.

Notes

_____

_____

_____

_____

_____

_____

_____

_____

_____

_____

DONALD TRUMP

- YOU HAVE TO THINK ANYWAY; WHY NOT THINK BIG?
- I TRY TO LEARN FROM THE PAST, BUT I PLAN FOR THE FUTURE BY FOCUSING EXCLUSIVELY ON THE PRESENT. THAT'S WHERE THE FUN IS.
- ONLY THOSE WHO DARE TO FAIL GREATLY CAN EVER ACHIEVE GREATLY.

Notes

_____

_____

_____

_____

_____

_____

_____

_____

_____

_____

JACKSON BROWN

OUR CHARACTER IS WHAT WE DO WHEN
WE THINK NO ONE IS LOOKING.

Notes

_____

_____

_____

_____

_____

_____

_____

_____

_____

_____

WALTER BENJAMIN

GIFTS MUST AFFECT THE RECEIVER TO
THE POINT OF SHOCK.

Notes

_____

_____

_____

_____

_____

_____

_____

_____

_____

_____

WALT WHITMAN

SUCCESS IS WITHIN THE INDIVIDUAL
NOT THE INSTITUTION.

Notes

_____

_____

_____

_____

_____

_____

_____

_____

_____

TOM BROKAW
(NBC news anchor)

IT IS NOT ENOUGH TO WIRE THE HEART
IF YOU SHORT CIRCUIT THE SOUL.
TECHNOLOGY WITHOUT HEART IS NOT
ENOUGH.

Notes

_____

_____

_____

_____

_____

_____

_____

_____

_____

_____

HENRY DAVID THOREAU

GO CONFIDENTLY IN THE DIRECTION
OF YOUR DREAMS. LIVE THE LIFE YOU'VE
IMAGINED.

Notes

_____

_____

_____

_____

_____

_____

_____

_____

_____

201

HENRY MACKAY
(Best selling author and business man)

IF I HAD TO NAME THE SINGLE ATTRIBUTE THAT DEFINES THE MOST SUCCESSFUL PEOPLE IT'S THEIR ABILITY TO NETWORK.

Notes

_____

_____

_____

_____

_____

_____

_____

_____

_____

_____

ELIJAH BERNARD JORDAN

- YOU CANNOT HAVE A FUTURE YOU HAVE NO KNOWLEDGE ABOUT, THE FUTURE IS BASED ON THE KNOWLEDGE YOU HAVE FROM WITHIN.
- TRUTH BRINGS GREAT REWARDS WHENEVER COMPROMISE IS REFUSED.
- YOU ONLY GROW BASED ON WHAT YOU KNOW, THAT'S WHY KNOWLEDGE IS SO IMPORTANT.

Notes

_____

_____

_____

_____

_____

_____

_____

_____

_____

BISHOP JULIO CAESAR

MORE GREAT THINGS ARE DONE THROUGH WISDOM THAN THROUGH INTELLIGENCE.

Notes

_____

_____

_____

_____

_____

_____

_____

_____

_____

DAVID J. SCHWATZ

- YOU MUST FIRST BE A BELIEVER BEFORE YOU CAN BECOME AN ACHIEVER.
- SEIZE THE MOMENT ! THERE ARE CERTAIN OPPORTUNITIES THAT ONLY COME ONCE IN A LIFETIME.

Notes

_____

_____

_____

_____

_____

_____

_____

_____

_____

_____

PHILIP SIDNEY

IN THE PERFORMANCE OF A GOOD
ACTION, A MAN NOT ONLY BENEFITS
HIMSELF, BUT HE CONFERS A BLESSING
ON OTHERS.

Notes

_____

_____

_____

_____

_____

_____

_____

_____

_____

_____

WILLIAM P. MERILL

UNLESS YOU GIVE YOURSELF TO SOME
GREAT CAUSE YOU HAVEN'T EVEN BEGUN
TO LIVE.

Notes

_____

_____

_____

_____

_____

_____

_____

_____

_____

_____

CHARLES C. G. TRUMBULL

THOSE WHO ARE READIEST TO TRUST GOD WITHOUT OTHER EVIDENCE THAN HIS WORD ALWAYS RECEIVE THE GREATEST NUMBER OF VISIBLE EVIDENCES OF HIS LOVE.

Notes

_____

_____

_____

_____

_____

_____

_____

_____

_____

_____

MARTIN GRIMES

WE DON'T KNOW WHO WE ARE UNTIL
WE SEE WHAT WE CAN DO.

Notes

_____

_____

_____

_____

_____

_____

_____

_____

_____

_____

JOEL OSTEEN

- CHOOSING TO BE POSITIVE AND HAVING A GRATEFUL ATTITUDE IS GOING TO DETERMINE HOW YOU'RE GOING TO LIVE YOUR LIFE.
- GOD DIDN'T MAKE A MISTAKE WHEN HE MADE YOU. YOU NEED TO SEE YOURSELF AS GOD SEES YOU.

Notes

_____

_____

_____

_____

_____

_____

_____

_____

_____

_____

JOHN MCCAIN

- WE CANNOT FOREVER HIDE THE TRUTH ABOUT OURSELVES, FROM OURSELVES.
- WAR IS WRETCHED BEYOND DESCRIPTION, AND ONLY A FOOL OR A FRAUD COULD SENTIMENTALISE IT'S CRUEL REALITY.
- WE CANNOT FOREVER HIDE THE TRUTH ABOUT OURSELVES, FROM OURSELVES.

Notes

ELVIS PRESLEY

- AMBITION IS A DREAM WITH A V8 ENGINE
- I HAVE NO USE FOR BODY GUARDS BUT I HAVE A VERY SPECIFIC USE FOR TWO HIGHLY TRAINED CERTIFIED PUBLIC ASSISTANT
- I KEEP A LEVEL HEAD. YOU HAVE TO BE CAREFUL OUT IN THE WORLD. IT IS SO EASY TO GET TURNED

Notes

_____

_____

_____

_____

_____

_____

_____

_____

_____

_____

NELSON MANDELA

- THE SUCCESSFUL MAN IS THE AVERAGE MAN WHO MAINTAINS HIS FOCUS.
- THE BRAVE MAN IS NOT HIM WHO DOES NOT FEEL AFRAID, BUT HE WHO CONQUERS THAT FEAR. I LEARNED THAT COURAGE WAS NOT THE ABSENCE OF FEAR, BUT THE TRIUMPH OVER IT
- FOR TO BE FREE IS NOT MERELY TO CAST OFF ONES' CHAINS, BUT TO LIVE IN A WAY THAT RESPECTS AND ENHANCES THE FREEDOM OF OTHERS
- A GOOD HEAD AND A GOOD HEART ARE ALWAYS A FORMIDABLE COMBINATION
- AND AS WE LET OUR OWN LIGHT SHINE, WE UNCONSCIOUSLY GIVE OTHER PEOPLE PERMISSION TO DO THE SAME.

Notes

225

KWAME NKRUMAH

- REVOLUTIONS ARE BROUGHT ABOUT BY MEN, BY MEN WHO THINK AS MEN OF ACTION AND ACT AS MEN OF THOUGHT.
- AS A NATION IT IS FAR BETTER TO GOVERN OR MISGOVERN YOURSELF THAN TO BE GOVERNED BY ANYBODY ELSE
- WE PREFER SELF GOVERNMENT WITH DANGER TO SERVITUDE IN TRANQUILITY.

Notes

GEORGE BERNARD SHAW

PROGRESS IS IMPOSSIBLE WITHOUT CHANGE, AND THOSE WHO CANNOT CHANGE THEIR MINDS CANNOT CHANGE ANYTHING.

Notes

_____

_____

_____

_____

_____

_____

_____

_____

_____

_____

BEN CARSON

- I THINK OF SUCCESS AS REACHING BEYOND OURSELVES AND HELPING OTHER PEOPLE IN SPECIFIC WAYS.
- WHAT IS IMPORTANT, WHAT I CONSIDER SUCCESS IS THAT WE MAKE A CONTRIBUTION TO OUR WORLD

Notes

_____

_____

_____

_____

_____

_____

_____

_____

_____

_____

BERTRAND RUSSELL

UNLESS YOU ASSUME A GOD, THE
QUESTION OF LIFE'S PURPOSE IS
MEANINGLESS.

Notes

_____

_____

_____

_____

_____

_____

_____

_____

_____

NNAMDI AZIKIWE (Statesman)

ORIGINALITY IS THE ESSENCE OF TRUE
SCHOLARSHIP. CREATIVITY IS THE SOUL
OF THE TRUE SCHOLAR.

Notes

235

BARACK OBAMA

- CHANGE WILL NOT COME IF WE WAIT FOR SOME OTHER PERSON OR SOME OTHER TIME. WE ARE THE ONES WE'VE BEEN WAITING FOR. WE ARE THE CHANGE WE SEEK.
- FOCUSING YOUR LIFE SOLELY ON MAKING A BUCK SHOWS A CERTAIN POVERTY OF AMBITION. IT ASKS TOO LITTLE OF YOURSELF BECAUSE IT'S ONLY WHEN YOU HITCH YOUR WAGON TO SOMETHING LARGER THAN YOURSELF THAT YOU REALISE YOUR TRUE POTENTIAL.

Notes

_____

_____

_____

_____

_____

_____

_____

_____

_____

_____

FREDERICK LANGBRIDGE

TWO MEN LOOK OUT THROUGH THE
SAME BARS, ONE SEES THE MUD AND
ONE THE STARS.

Notes

_____

_____

_____

_____

_____

_____

_____

_____

_____

_____

NORMAL VINCENT PEALE

- THE WORLD IS EXTREMELY INTERESTING TO A POSITIVE PERSON.
- GIVING IS A GREAT JOY PRODUCER.

Notes

_____

_____

_____

_____

_____

_____

_____

_____

_____

_____

NICOLLO MACHIAVELLI

- BENEFITS SHOULD BE CONFERRED GRADUALLY; AND IN THAT WAY THEY WILL TASTE BETTER.
- HATRED IS GAINED AS MUCH BY GOOD WORKS AS BY EVIL.
- ENTERPRENEURS ARE SIMPLY THOSE WHO UNDERSTAND THAT THERE IS LITTLE DIFFERENCE BETWEEN OBSTACLES AND OPPORTUNITY AND ARE ABLE TO TURN BOTH TO THEIR ADVANTAGE.

Notes

_____

_____

_____

_____

_____

_____

_____

_____

_____

_____

_____

JOHN L. MASON

- CROWS FLY IN GROUPS EAGLES FLY ALONE.
- FAILURE IS SUCCESS TURNED INSIDE OUT.
- OBSERVE THE AVERAGE, DO THE OPPOSITE.

Notes

SPENCER SILVER
(Inventor of the post it notes)

IF I HAD THOUGHT ABOUT IT I WOULDN'T HAVE DONE THE EXPERIMENT. THE LITERATURE WAS FULL OF EXAMPLES THAT SAID YOU CAN'T DO THIS.

Notes

_____

_____

_____

_____

_____

_____

_____

_____

_____

_____

MADAME GUYION

IT IS THE FIRE OF SUFFERING THAT BRINGS
FORTH THE GOLD OF GODLINESS.

Notes

ANAIS NIN

WE DON'T SEE THINGS AS THEY ARE, WE SEE THEM AS WE ARE.

Notes

_____

_____

_____

_____

_____

_____

_____

_____

_____

_____

RICK WARREN

LIVING FOR GOD'S GLORY IS THE GREATEST ACHIEVEMENT WE CAN ACCOMPLISH WITH OUR LIVES.

Notes

_____

_____

_____

_____

_____

_____

_____

_____

_____

THOMAS CARLYLE

THE MAN WITHOUT A PURPOSE IS LIKE A SHIP WITHOUT A RUDDER-A WAIF, A NOTHING, A NO MAN.

Notes

MARTIN LUTHER

WE GROW THROUGH TEMPTATION, MY
TEMPTATIONS HAVE BEEN MY MASTERS
IN DIVINITY.

Notes

_____

_____

_____

_____

_____

_____

_____

_____

_____

_____

DANISH PROVERB

WHAT YOU ARE IS GODS GIFT TO YOU;
WHAT YOU DO WITH YOURSELF IS YOUR
GIFT TO GOD.

Notes

_____

_____

_____

_____

_____

_____

_____

_____

_____

_____

GEORGE BERNARD SHAW

PEOPLE WHO WAIT FOR PERFECT CONDITIONS BEFORE THEY DO ANYTHING WILL NEVER GET MUCH DONE.

Notes

_____

_____

_____

_____

_____

_____

_____

_____

_____

_____

JAMES MERRITT

- KINDNESS IS THE SWEETNER TO THE COFFEE OF MARRIAGE.
- WITH A LITTLE KINDNESS YOU CAN KILL HARD FEELINGS.

Notes

_____

_____

_____

_____

_____

_____

_____

_____

_____

_____

ROBERT TILTON

THE MORE YOU DO WITH WHAT YOU
KNOW DETERMINES HOW FAR YOU GO.

Notes

_____

_____

_____

_____

_____

_____

_____

_____

_____

_____

JACK NICKLAUS

FRIENDSHIP WITH ONES SELF IS ALL
IMPORTANT BECAUSE WITHOUT IT ONE
CANNOT BE FRIENDS WITH ANYONE
ELSE IN THE WORLD.

Notes

_____

_____

_____

_____

_____

_____

_____

_____

_____

_____

JOHN D. ROCKFELLAR

CHARITY IS INJURIOUS UNLESS IT HELPS THE RECIPIENT TO BECOME INDEPENDENT OF IT.

Notes

_____

_____

_____

_____

_____

_____

_____

_____

_____

_____

BRUCE BARTON

MOST SUCCESSFUL MEN HAVE NOT
ACHIEVED THEIR DISTINCTION BY
SOME NEW TALENT OR OPPORTUNITY
PRESENTED TO THEM. THEY HAVE
DEVELOPED THE OPPORTUNITY AT
HAND.

Notes

_____

_____

_____

_____

_____

_____

_____

_____

_____

_____

WARREN BUFFET

- PROFIT FROM FOLLY RATHER THAN BE PART OF IT.
- IF YOU WAIT TILL YOU SEE THE ROBIN, SPRING WILL BE OVER.

Notes

_____

_____

_____

_____

_____

_____

_____

_____

_____

_____

WILLIAM NEWTON CLARKE

FAITH IS DARING THE SOUL TO GO
BEYOND WHAT THE EYES CAN SEE.

Notes

THOMAS AQUINAS

TO ONE WHO HAS FAITH, NO
EXPLANATION IS NECESSARY. TO ONE
WITHOUT FAITH, NO EXPLANATION IS
POSSIBLE.

Notes

_____

_____

_____

_____

_____

_____

_____

_____

_____

_____

CONFUCIOUS

THREE THINGS CANNOT LONG BE HIDDEN; THE SUN, THE MOON, AND THE TRUTH.

Notes

_____

_____

_____

_____

_____

_____

_____

_____

_____

_____

JON ENGLISH

YOU CAN LAY DOWN AND DIE, OR YOU
CAN GET UP AND FIGHT, BUT THATS IT
THERE'S NO TURNING BACK.

Notes

CHARLES DE GAULLE

- FACED WITH CRISIS THE MAN OF CHARACTER FALLS BACK ON HIMSELF. HE IMPROVES HIS OWN STAMP OF ACTION, TAKES RESPONSIBILITY FOR IT, MAKES IT HIS OWN.
- PERMANENCE, PERSERVERANCE AND PERSISTENCE IN SPITE OF ALL OBSTACLES, DISCOURAGEMENT, AND ITS POSSIBILITIES: IT IS THIS, THAT IN ALL THINGS DISTINGUISHES THE STRONG SOUL FROM THE WEAK.

Notes

RABBI YEHUDA PRERO

WHAT WE SEE, WHAT WE CAN VISUALISE
IS OFTEN WHAT WE GET.

Notes

_____

_____

_____

_____

_____

_____

_____

_____

_____

_____

TODD COONTZ

THE CLOSER WE WALK TO THE SHEPHERD
THE FARTHER WE ARE FROM THE WOLF,
WE ALL NEED MENTORS IN OUR LIVES.

Notes

_____

_____

_____

_____

_____

_____

_____

_____

_____

_____

CHRISTOPHER COLUMBUS

THE WORLD IS ROUND AND THE PLACE
WHICH MAY SEEM LIKE THE END MAY
ALSO BE THE BEGINNING, NEVER GIVE
UP.

Notes

OSCAR WILDE

MOST PEOPLE ARE OTHER PEOPLE.
THEIR THOUGHTS ARE SOMEONE ELSES
OPINION, THEIR LIVES A MIMCRY, THEIR
PASSIONS A QUOTATION.

Notes

_____

_____

_____

_____

_____

_____

_____

_____

_____

_____

ERIC GLENN

THE MOST IMPORTANT SINGLE FACTOR IN INDIVIDUAL SUCCESS IS COMMITMENT.

Notes

_____

_____

_____

_____

_____

_____

_____

_____

_____

_____

ROUSSEAU SWISS

DO NOT JUDGE AND YOU WILL NEVER BE
MISTAKEN.

Notes

_____

_____

_____

_____

_____

_____

_____

_____

_____

_____

WILLIAM J. JOHNSON

THE MOST SIGNIFICANT CHANGE IN A PERSONS LIFE IS A CHANGE OF ATTITUDE-RIGHT ATTITUDES PRODUCE RIGHT ACTION.

Notes

_____

_____

_____

_____

_____

_____

_____

_____

_____

_____

SOPHOCLES

HEAVEN NEVER HELPS THE PERSON WHO
WILL NOT ACT.

Notes

_____

_____

_____

_____

_____

_____

_____

_____

_____

EDWIN LEWIS COLE

- YOU DONT DROWN BY FALLING IN THE WATER; YOU DROWN BY STAYING THERE.
- BRAVERY IS BEING THE ONLY ONE WHO KNOWS YOUR AFRAID.
- CHARACTER IS MORE IMPORTANT THAN TALENT.

Notes

_____

_____

_____

_____

_____

_____

_____

_____

_____

_____

_____

Dr. JAMES DOBSON

- THE THING THAT GUARANTEES A FUTURE FOR YOUR CHILDREN IS NOT EDUCATION OR MONEY, BUT THE EXAMPLE OF UNION BETWEEN PARENTS .
- A COUPLE ARE LIKE A TREE AND THEIR CHILDREN LIKE THE FRUIT OF THAT TREE. IF THE TREE IS GOOD THE FRUIT WILL ALSO BE GOOD.

Notes

_____

_____

_____

_____

_____

_____

_____

_____

_____

_____

JOYCE MEYER

IT IS NOT ENOUGH TO JUST SPEAK CORRECTLY; ABOVE ALL YOU MUST THINK CORRECTLY.

Notes

_____

_____

_____

_____

_____

_____

_____

_____

_____

_____

PLATO

PRAYER IS SAYING WHATS IN YOUR HEART; ITS EXPRESSING THE FEELINGS OF YOUR SOUL TO GOD.

Notes

_____

_____

_____

_____

_____

_____

_____

_____

_____

_____

W. F KUMUYI

DESIRE, DETERMINATION, DISCIPLINE AND DILIGENCE ARE THE FOUR D'S THAT MAKE MEN SUCCESSFUL

Notes

_____

_____

_____

_____

_____

_____

_____

_____

_____

THEODORE ROOSEVELT

WHEN YOU PLAY, PLAY HARD, WHEN YOU
WORK, DON'T PLAY AT ALL.

Notes

_____

_____

_____

_____

_____

_____

_____

_____

_____

_____

KENNETH COPELAND

YOU ARE NOT BLESSED BECAUSE YOU HAVE MONEY, YOU HAVE MONEY BECAUSE YOU ARE BLESSED.

Notes

_____

_____

_____

_____

_____

_____

_____

_____

_____

_____

ROY DISNEY

WHEN YOUR VALUES ARE CLEAR TO YOU,
MAKING DECISIONS BECOME EASIER.

Notes

_____

_____

_____

_____

_____

_____

_____

_____

_____

_____

DAVID J. SCHWARTZ

HOW BIG WE THINK DETERMINES THE
SIZE OF OUR ACCOMPLISHMENTS.

_____

_____

_____

_____

_____

_____

_____

_____

_____

_____

J.M POWER

IF YOU WANT TO MAKE YOUR DREAMS
COME TRUE THE FIRST THING YOU HAVE
TO DO IS WAKE UP.

Notes

_____

_____

_____

_____

_____

_____

_____

_____

_____

GENERAL GEORGE S. PATTON

YOU NEED TO OVERCOME THE TUG OF
PEOPLE AGAINST YOU AS YOU REACH FOR
HIGH GOALS.

Notes

_____

_____

_____

_____

_____

_____

_____

_____

_____

_____

_____

GEOFFRY F. ALBERT

THE MOST IMPORTANT THING ABOUT
GOALS IS HAVING ONE.

Notes

_____

_____

_____

_____

_____

_____

_____

_____

_____

_____

JEFFREY ARCHER

WE ALL MAKE MISTAKES BUT ONE HAS
TO MOVE ON.

Notes

JULIUS ERVING

GOALS DETERMINE WHAT YOU'RE GOING TO BE.

Notes

_____

_____

_____

_____

_____

_____

_____

_____

_____

_____

RONALD REGAN

FREEDOM PROSPERS WHEN FAITH IS
VIBRANT AND THE RULE OF LAW UNDER
GOD IS ACKNOWLEDGED.

Notes

LORD CHESTERFIELD

BE WISER THAN OTHER PEOPLE IF YOU
CAN, BUT DO NOT TELL THEM SO.

Notes

_____

_____

_____

_____

_____

_____

_____

_____

_____

_____

JACK NICKLAUS

RESOLVE NEVER TO QUIT, NEVER TO GIVE UP, NO MATTER THE SITUATION.

Notes

_____

_____

_____

_____

_____

_____

_____

_____

_____

_____

SIDNEY NEWTON BREMMER

- PROMPT DECISION AND WHOLE-SOULED ACTION SWEEP THE WORLD BEFORE GREAT ACHIEVERS.
- THERE NEVER WAS A MAN WHO ACHIEVED PECULIAR EMINENCE WHO DID NOT DO IT BY ADVANCING UPON A PATH THAT HE MADE AS HE WENT ALONG.
- IT IS THE BRIGHT AND CHEERFUL SPIRIT THAT WINS THE FINAL TRIUMPH.
- CHARACTER IS WHAT A MAN IS, REPUTATION IS WHAT HE THINKS HE IS.
- PURPOSE MUST BE FOLLOWED BY ACTION. GREAT MEN NEVER WAIT FOR OPPORTUNITIES; THEY MAKE THEM

Notes

_____

_____

_____

_____

_____

_____

_____

_____

_____

_____

_____

GALILEO

- ALL TRUTHS ARE EASY TO UNDERSTAND ONCE THEY ARE DISCOVERED, THE POINT IS TO DISCOVER THEM
- I DO NOT FEEL OBLIGED THAT THE SAME GOD WHO HAS ENDOWED US WITH SENSE, REASON AND INTELLECT HAS INTENDED US TO FORGO THEIR USE.

Notes

_____

_____

_____

_____

_____

_____

_____

_____

_____

MICHAEL FARADAY (Physicist)

THE IMPORTANT THING IS TO KNOW
HOW TO TAKE ALL THINGS QUIETLY.

Notes

GEORGE WASHINGTON
(first President of America)

A SLENDER AQUAINTANCE WITH THE WORLD MUST CONVINCE EVERYMAN THAT ACTIONS, NOT WORDS, ARE THE TRUE CRITERION OF THE ATTACHMENT OF FRIENDS.

Notes

_____

_____

_____

_____

_____

_____

_____

_____

_____

_____

JAMES WATT
(Developer of Steam)

A LIE CAN RUN AROUND THE WORLD BEFORE
TRUTH CAN GET IT'S BOOTS ON.

Notes

_____

_____

_____

_____

_____

_____

_____

_____

_____

_____

JULIUS CAESAR

COWARDS DIE MANY TIMES BEFORE
THEIR ACTUAL DEATHS.

Notes

_____

_____

_____

_____

_____

_____

_____

_____

_____

_____

SOCRATES

- LET HIM THAT WILL MOVE THE WORLD FIRST MOVE HIMSELF.
- CONTENTMENT IS NATURAL WEALTH. LUXURY IS ARTIFICIAL POVERTY.

Notes

HORACE

- CALAMITIES OFTEN REVEAL GENIUS.
- ADVERSITY REVEALS GENIUS, PROSPERITY CONCEALS IT.
- GOOD SENSE IS BOTH THE FIRST PRINCIPAL AND THE PARENT SOURCE OF GOOD WRITTING.

Notes

_____

_____

_____

_____

_____

_____

_____

_____

_____

_____

PERICLES

- HAVING KNOWLEDGE BUT LACKING THE POWER TO EXPRESS IT CLEARLY IS NO BETTER THAN EVER HAVING ANY IDEA AT ALL.
- WHAT YOU LEAVE BEHIND IS NOT WHAT IS ENGRAVED IN STONE MONUMENTS, BUT WHAT IS WOVEN INTO THE LIVES OF OTHERS.

Notes

_____

_____

_____

_____

_____

_____

_____

_____

_____

_____

CLAUDIUS (Roman Emperor)

EVERY INDIVIDUAL TO A GOOD DEGREE IS THE ARCHITECT OF HIS OWN FORTUNE.

Notes

_____

_____

_____

_____

_____

_____

_____

_____

_____

OVID

- A PRINCE SHOULD BE SLOW TO PUNISH AND QUICK TO REWARD.
- COURAGE CONQUERS ALL THINGS IT EVEN GIVES STRENGTH TO THE BODY.
- CHANCE IS ALWAYS POWERFUL. LET YOUR HOOK ALWAYS BE CAST; IN THE POOL WHERE YOU LEAST EXPECT IT, THERE WILL BE FISH.
- A NEW IDEA IS DELICATE. IT CAN BE KILLED BY A SNEER OR A YAWN; IT CAN BE STABBED TO DEATH BY A QUIP AND WORRIED TO DEATH BY A FROWN ON THE RIGHT MAN'S BOW.

Notes

_____

_____

_____

_____

_____

_____

_____

_____

_____

_____

SIDNEY POITIER

BUT I ALWAYS HAD THE ABILITY TO SAY NO. THAT'S HOW I CALLED MY OWN SHOTS.

Notes

_____

_____

_____

_____

_____

_____

_____

_____

_____

_____

SALVADOR DALI
(Artist and Designer)

- HAVE NO FEAR OF PERFECTION - YOU'LL NEVER REACH IT.
- INTELLIGENCE WITHOUT AMBITION IS A BIRD WITHOUT WINGS.

Notes

_____

_____

_____

_____

_____

_____

_____

_____

BURT RUTAN

- WE NEED AFFORDABLE SPACE TRAVEL TO INSPIRE OUR YOUTH, TO LET THEM KNOW THAT THEY CAN EXPERIENCE THEIR DREAMS, THAT THEY CAN SET SIGNIFICANT GOALS AND BE IN A POSITION TO LEAD US ALL TO FUTURE PROGRESS IN EXPLORATION, DISCOVERY AND FUN.
- TO STUMBLE INTO A BREAKTHROUGH YOU'RE GOING TO BE MORE CREATIVE, MORE INNOVATIVE AND HAVE A LOT MORE ABILITY.
- TESTING LEADS TO FAILURE, AND FAILURE LEADS TO UNDERSTANDING.

Notes

_____

_____

_____

_____

_____

_____

_____

_____

_____

_____

DOROTHY THOMPSON

- ONLY WHEN WE ARE NO LONGER AFRAID DO WE BEGIN TO LIVE.
- HATE SMOLDERS AND EVENTUALLY DESTROYS, NOT THE HATED BUT THE HATER.

Notes

_____

_____

_____

_____

_____

_____

_____

_____

_____

PAUL SAMUELSON
(Nobel Laurent, MIT)

SOONER OR LATER THE INTERNET WILL
BECOME PROFITABLE. IT'S AN OLD STORY
PLAYED BEFORE BY CANALS, RAIL ROADS
AND AUTOMOBILES.

Notes

_____

_____

_____

_____

_____

_____

_____

_____

_____

_____

LOUIS PASTEUR

- CHANCE FAVOURS ONLY THE PREPARED MIND.
- WHEN I APPROACH A CHILD HE INSPIRES ME IN TWO SENTIMENTS; TENDERNESS FOR WHAT HE IS, AND RESPECT FOR WHAT HE MAY BECOME.
- LET ME TELL YOU THE SECRET THAT HAS LED ME TO MY GOAL. MY STRENGTH LIES SOLELY IN MY TENACITY.

Notes

_____

_____

_____

_____

_____

_____

_____

_____

_____

JOHN LOCKE
(British Philosopher)

- A SOUND MIND IN A SOUND BODY, IS SHORT, BUT FULL OF DESCRIPTION OF A HAPPY STATE IN THIS WORLD: HE WHO HAS THIS TWO, HAS LITTLE TO WISH FOR; AND HE THAT WANTS EITHER OF THEM, WILL BE LITTLE THE BETTER FOR ANYTHING ELSE.

- THE BIBLE IS ONE OF THE GREATEST BLESSINGS BESTOWED BY GOD ON THE CHILDREN OF MEN. IT HAS GOD AS ITS AUTHOR; SALVATION FOR ITS END, AND TRUTH WITHOUT ANY MIXTURE FOR ITS MATTER. IT IS ALL PURE.

Notes

_____

_____

_____

_____

_____

_____

_____

_____

_____

_____

ARISTOTLE ONASIS

- TO SUCCEED IN BUSINESS IT IS NECESSARY TO MAKE OTHERS SEE THINGS THE WAY YOU SEE THEM.
- IT'S DURING OUR DARKEST MOMENTS WE MUST FOCUS TO SEE THE LIGHT.
- THE SECRET OF BUSINESS IS TO KNOW SOMETHING NOBODY ELSE KNOWS.

Notes

_____

_____

_____

_____

_____

_____

_____

_____

_____

SIR THOMAS MOORE

THOSE WHO PLOT THE DESTRUCTION OF OTHERS OFTEN PERISH IN THE ATTEMPT.

Notes

_____

_____

_____

_____

_____

_____

_____

_____

_____

_____

RENE DESCARTES

IT IS NOT ENOUGH TO HAVE A GOOD
MIND THE MAIN THING IS TO USE IT
WELL.

Notes

EMMANUEL KANT

BY A LIE, A MAN...ANNIHILATES HIS DIGNITY AS A MAN.

Notes

PYTHAGORAS

- DO NOT SAY A LITTLE IN MANY WORDS
  BUT A GREAT DEAL IN A FEW.
- REST SATISFIED WITH DOING WELL ,
  AND LEAVE OTHERS TO TALK OF YOU
  AS THEY PLEASE.

Notes

_____

_____

_____

_____

_____

_____

_____

_____

_____

_____

WILLIAM WILBERFORCE

- MEN OF AUTHORITY AND INFLUENCE MAY PROMOTE GOOD MORALS. LET THEM IN THEIR SEVERAL STATIONS ENCOURAGE VIRTUE...LET THEM FAVOR AND TAKE PART IN ANY PLANS WHICH MAY BE FORMED FOR THE ADVANCEMENT OF MORALITY.
- LET EVERYONE REGULATE HIS CONDUCT... BY THE GOLDEN RULE OF DOING TO OTHERS AS IN SIMILAR CIRCUMSTANCES WE WILL HAVE THEM DO TO US, AND THE PATH OF DUTY WILL BE CLEAR BEFORE HIM.

Notes

_____

_____

_____

_____

_____

_____

_____

_____

_____

_____

BILLY GRAHAM

- A CHILD WHO IS ALLOWED TO BE DISRESPECTFUL TO HIS PARENTS WILL NOT HAVE TRUE RESPECT FOR ANYONE.
- COMFORT AND PROSPERITY HAVE NEVER ENRICHED THE WORLD AS ADVERSITY HAS.

Notes

_____

_____

_____

_____

_____

_____

_____

_____

_____

_____

KARL MAX

- EXPERIENCE PRAISES THE MOST HAPPY THE ONE WHO MADE THE MOST PEOPLE HAPPY.
- NOTHING CAN HAVE VALUE WITHOUT BEING AN OBJECT OF UTILITY.

Notes

_____

_____

_____

_____

_____

_____

_____

_____

ARNOLD SCHWARZENEGGER

BODY BUILDING IS JUST LIKE ANY
OTHER SPORT. TO BE SUCCESSFUL YOU
MUST DEDICATE YOURSELF 100% TO
YOUR TRAINING, DIET AND MENTAL
APPROACH.

Notes

_____

_____

_____

_____

_____

_____

_____

_____

_____

_____

OBAFEMI AWOLOWO (STATEMAN)

- I OWE MY SUCCESS TO THREE MAJOR THINGS IN LIFE, THE GRACE OF GOD, A SPARTAN SELF DISCIPLINE, AND A GOOD WIFE.
- VIOLENCE NEVER SETTLES ANYTHING RIGHT: APART FROM INJURING YOUR OWN SOUL, IT INJURES THE BEST CAUSE. IT LINGERS ON LONG AFTER THE OBJECT OF HATE HAS DISAPPEARED FROM THE SCENE TO PLAGUE THE LIVES OF THOSE WHO HAVE EMPLOYED IT AGAINST THEIR FOES.

Notes

_____

_____

_____

_____

_____

_____

_____

_____

_____

_____

JOHN JOHNSON
(Founder Ebony Magazine)

- FAILURE IS A WORD WE MUST NOT ACCEPT.
- HARD WORK, DEDICATION AND PERSEVERANCE WILL OVERCOME ALMOST ANY PREJUDICE AND OPEN ALMOST ANY DOOR.

Notes

_____

_____

_____

_____

_____

_____

_____

_____

_____

_____

JESSE JACKSON

TIME IS NEUTRAL AND DOES NOT
CHANGE THINGS. WITH COURAGE AND
INITIATIVE LEADERS CHANGE THINGS.

Notes

BOOTH TARKINGTON

AN IDEAL WIFE IS ANY WOMAN WHO HAS
AN IDEAL HUSBAND.

Notes

_____

_____

_____

_____

_____

_____

_____

_____

_____

_____

ARIEL AND WILL DURANT

THE FAMILY IS THE NUCLEUS 'OF
CIVILIZATION.

Notes

CARL SANDBURG

A BABY IS GOD'S OPINION THAT THE
WORLD SHOULD GO ON.

Notes

_____

_____

_____

_____

_____

_____

_____

_____

_____

_____

_____

CONFUCIOUS

GOVERN A FAMILY AS YOU WOULD COOK
A SMALL FISH – VERY GENTLY.

Notes

_____

_____

_____

_____

_____

_____

_____

_____

_____

_____

ALBERT CAMUS

NOTHING IS MORE DESPICABLE THAN
RESPECT BASED ON FEAR.

Notes

_____

_____

_____

_____

_____

_____

_____

_____

_____

M.K.O ABIOLA
(Businessman and Nigerian statesman)

THE LONGER THE BATTLE AHEAD THE
SWEETER THE GRAPES OF VICTORY.

Notes

OLUSEGUN OBASANJO
(Statesman and former Nigerian President)

UNFORTUNATELY, THE TRUE FORCE WHICH PROPELS OUR ENDLESS POLITICAL DISPUTES, OUR CONSTANT STRUGGLE FOR POLITICAL ADVANTAGE, IS OFTEN NOT OUR BURNING CONCERN FOR DEMOCRACY , IT IS OFTEN OF OUR DEDICATION TO THE PRINCIPLE OF THE RULE OF LAW.

Notes

_____

_____

_____

_____

_____

_____

_____

_____

_____

_____

MYLES MUNROE

- YOU HAVE TO BELIEVE AND WORK YOUR PLAN INTO EXISTENCE.
- IF YOU WANT TO SUCCEED, STRIKE OUT ON NEW PATHS.
- REACH BEYOND YOUR GRASP. YOUR BODY IS NOT YOUR FULL POTENTIAL.

Notes

_____

_____

_____

_____

_____

_____

_____

_____

_____

_____

JOHN C. MAXWELL

- GOOD EXECUTIVES NEVER PUT OFF UNTIL TOMORROW WHAT THEY CAN GET SOMEONE ELSE TO DO TODAY.
- A LEADER IS ONE WHO KNOWS THE WAY, GOES THE WAY AND SHOWS THE WAY.

Notes

_____

_____

_____

_____

_____

_____

_____

_____

_____

_____

RICHARD M. DEVOS
(Co-founder of the Amway Cooperation)

- IF YOU HAVE A DREAM, GIVE IT A CHANCE TO HAPPEN.
- THE EASIEST THING TO FIND ON GOD'S GREEN EARTH IS SOMEONE TO TELL YOU ALL THE THINGS YOU CANNOT DO.
- THE ONLY THING THAT STANDS BETWEEN A MAN AND WHAT HE WANTS FROM LIFE IS OFTEN MERELY THE WILL TO TRY IT AND THE FAITH TO BELIEVE THAT IT IS POSSIBLE.

Notes

Soichiro Honda
(Founder of Honda cars)

- SUCCESS IS 99% FAILURE.
- IF YOU HIRE ONLY PEOPLE YOU UNDERSTAND, THE COMPANY WILL NEVER GET PEOPLE BETTER THAN YOU ARE. ALWAYS REMEMBER THAT YOU OFTEN FIND OUTSTANDING PEOPLE AMONG THOSE YOU DON'T PARTICULARLY LIKE.

Notes

PELE (Legendary Brazilian football player)

- SUCCESS IS NO ACCIDENT. IT IS HARD WORK, PERSEVERANCE, LEARNING, STUDYING, SACRIFICE, AND MOST OF ALL, LOVE OF WHAT YOU ARE DOING OR LEARNING TO DO.
- ENTHUSIASM IS EVERYTHING. IT MUST BE TAUT AND VIBRATING LIKE A GUITAR STRING.

Notes

MICHAEL DELL
(Founder of Dell computers)

IT'S CUSTOMERS THAT MADE DELL GREAT IN THE FIRST PLACE, AND IF WE ARE SMART ENOUGH AND QUICK ENOUGH TO LISTEN TO CUSTOMER NEEDS, WE'LL SUCCEED.

Notes

SAM WALTON
(Founder Walmart Stores)

- CAPITAL ISN'T SCARCE; VISION IS.
- OUTSTANDING LEADERS GO OUT OF THEIR WAY TO BOOST THE SELF-ESTEEM OF THEIR PERSONNEL. IF PEOPLE BELIEVE IN THEMSELVES, IT'S AMAZING WHAT THEY CAN ACCOMPLISH.

Notes

421

PHILIP GREEN
(Founder of Top Shop)

BE BRAVE BUT TAKE A VIEW. LET IT BE AN
EDUCATED VIEW. BE CAREFUL. DON'T BE
RECKLESS.

Notes

_____

_____

_____

_____

_____

_____

_____

_____

_____

_____

MICHAEL JACKSON

THE MEANING OF LIFE IS CONTAINED IN EVERY SINGLE FORM OF EXPRESSION. IT IS PRESENT IN THE INFINITY OF FORMS AND PHENOMENA THAT EXIST IN ALL OF CREATION.

Notes

MIGUEL DE CARVANTES

FAINT HEARTED MEN DONT WIN FAIR
LADIES.

Notes

_____

_____

_____

_____

_____

_____

_____

_____

_____

_____

_____

JIM ROHN

TIME IS MORE VALUABLE THAN MONEY. YOU CAN GET MORE MONEY, BUT YOU CANNOT GET MORE TIME.

Notes

_____

_____

_____

_____

_____

_____

_____

_____

_____

_____

VOLTAIRE

WHEN IT'S A QUESTION OF MONEY,
EVERYBODY IS OF THE SAME RELIGION.

Notes

_____

_____

_____

_____

_____

_____

_____

_____

_____

_____

OSCAR WILDE

WHEN I WAS YOUNG, I THOUGHT THAT
MONEY WAS THE MOST IMPORTANT
THING IN LIFE; NOW THAT I AM OLD, I
KNOW IT IS.

Notes

————————————————

————————————————

————————————————

————————————————

————————————————

————————————————

————————————————

————————————————

————————————————

————————————————

THOMAS ALVA EDISON

- IF WE DO ALL THE THINGS WE ARE CAPABLE OF DOING, WE WOULD LITERALLY ASTONISH OURSELVES.
- MANY OF LIFES FAILURE ARE PEOPLE WHO DID NOT REALISE HOW CLOSE THEY WERE TO SUCCESS WHEN THEY GAVE UP.
- THERE IS A BETTER WAY TO DO EVERYTHING. FIND IT.
- IF WE DO ALL THE THINGS WE ARE CAPABLE OF DOING, WE WOULD LITERALLY ASTONISH OURSELVES.

Notes

_____

_____

_____

_____

_____

_____

_____

_____

_____

_____

_____

SENECA

TO WISH TO BE WELL IS A PART OF
BECOMING WELL.

Notes

_____

_____

_____

_____

_____

_____

_____

_____

_____

_____

AUSTIN DACEY

GUTS ARE IMPORTANT. YOUR GUTS ARE WHAT DIGESTS THINGS. BUT IT'S YOUR BRAINS THAT TELLS YOU WHICH THINGS TO SWALLOW AND WHICH NOT TO SWALLOW.

Notes

_____

_____

_____

_____

_____

_____

_____

_____

_____

_____

BALTASAR GRACIAN

WITHOUT COURAGE , WISDOM BEARS
NO FRUIT.

Notes

_____

_____

_____

_____

_____

_____

_____

_____

_____

_____

LEE IACOCCA
(former C.E.O of Chrysler Motors)

- NO MATTER WHAT YOU HAVE DONE FOR YOURSELF OR HUMANITY, IF YOU CAN'T LOOK BACK ON HAVING GIVEN LOVE AND ATTENTION TO YOUR OWN FAMILY, WHAT HAVE YOU REALLY ACCOMPLISHED.
- SUCCESS LYES WITHIN INDIVIDUALS NOT THINGS, SUCCESS WILL COME OUT OF POSITIVE SOCIALISING.

Notes

_____

_____

_____

_____

_____

_____

_____

_____

_____

_____

BENJAMIN FRANKLIN

- A GOOD CONSCIENCE IS A CONTINUAL CHRISTMAS.
- A LEARNED BLOCK HEAD IS A GREATER BLOCK HEAD THAN AN ARROGANT ONE.

Notes

445

MOSHE DAYAN

- FREEDOM IS THE OXYGEN OF THE SOUL.
- IT'S TIME WE PLANNED OUR LIVES, AFTERALL WE ARE NOT CHILDREN.

Notes

_____

_____

_____

_____

_____

_____

_____

_____

_____

_____

VILLE VALO

WOMEN ARE ALWAYS BEAUTIFUL.

Notes

_____

_____

_____

_____

_____

_____

_____

_____

_____

_____

STEPHEN STILLS

THERE ARE THREE THINGS MEN CAN DO WITH WOMEN: LOVE THEM, SUFFER FOR THEM OR TURN THEM INTO LITERATURE.

Notes

451

ARTHUR CLARKE

THE ONLY WAY TO DISCOVER THE LIMITS
OF THE POSSIBLE IS TO GO BEYOND THEM
INTO THE IMPOSSIBLE.

Notes

_____

_____

_____

_____

_____

_____

_____

_____

_____

_____

HUGH PRATHER

THERE IS A TIME TO LET THINGS HAPPEN
AND A TIME TO MAKE THINGS HAPPEN.

Notes

_____

_____

_____

_____

_____

_____

_____

_____

_____

_____

JOHN SCULLEY

THE FUTURE BELONGS TO THOSE WHO
SEE POSSIBILITIES BEFORE THEY BECOME
OBVIOUS.

Notes

DR. O. C. APOKI

IT IS VERY SAD FOR LIFE TO LOCATE YOU
CLOSE TO WHAT AND WHERE YOU ARE
SUPPOSED TO BE AND YET BE VERY FAR
FROM IT. BUT FAILURE MIXED WITH
FAITH PRODUCES A FUTURE.

Notes

_____

_____

_____

_____

_____

_____

_____

_____

_____

_____

BILL WINSTON

YOU CAN START OUT WITH NOTHING AND END UP WITH EVERYTHING IF YOU ARE WILLING TO SERVE BY SOWING YOUR SERVICE AS A SEED.

Notes

―――――――――――――――――――――――――

―――――――――――――――――――――――――

―――――――――――――――――――――――――

―――――――――――――――――――――――――

―――――――――――――――――――――――――

―――――――――――――――――――――――――

―――――――――――――――――――――――――

―――――――――――――――――――――――――

―――――――――――――――――――――――――

―――――――――――――――――――――――――

STEVE HARVEY

WE DON'T GET ANYWHERE IF WE
DONT USE THE INFORMATION AND
KNOWLEDGE OF OTHERS.

Notes

_____

_____

_____

_____

_____

_____

_____

_____

_____

_____

DR UMA UKPAI

LIFE IS ALL ABOUT CELEBRATING AND
APPRECIATING OTHER PEOPLE.

Notes

_____

_____

_____

_____

_____

_____

_____

_____

_____

_____

MAYA ANGELOU

WE SPEND PRECIOUS HOURS FEARING THE INEVITABLE. IT WILL BE WISE TO USE THAT TIME ADORING OUR FAMILIES, CHERISHING OUR FRIENDS, AND LIVING OUR LIVES.

Notes

467

MARCEL BICH
(Founder of the BIC Corporation)

MY SUCCESS IS DUE TO MY REFUSAL TO
LISTEN TO ALMOST NO ONE'S ADVICE,
BUT MY OWN. WE HAVE TO BE FOCUSED
IN LIFE.

Notes

_____

_____

_____

_____

_____

_____

_____

_____

_____

SAMUEL JOHNSON

THOSE THAT HAVE DONE NOTHING
IN LIFE ARE NOT QUALIFIED TO JUDGE
THOSE THAT HAVE DONE LITTLE.

Notes

PHILIP ADAMS

UNLESS YOU ARE WILLING TO FAIL
MISERABLY AND HAVE ANOTHER GO,
SUCCESS WON'T HAPPEN.

Notes

_____

_____

_____

_____

_____

_____

_____

_____

_____

_____

JOSEPH CAMPBELL

OPPORTUNITIES TO FIND DEEPER
POWERS WITHIN OURSELVES COME ,
WHEN LIFE IS MOST CHALLENGING.

Notes

MAXWELL MALTZ

LOW SELF-ESTEEM IS LIKE DRIVING THROUGH LIFE WITH YOUR HAND-BREAK ON.

Notes

_____

_____

_____

_____

_____

_____

_____

_____

_____

_____

NEWT GINGRICH

PERSEVERANCE IS THE HARD WORK YOU
DO AFTER YOU GET TIRED OF DOING
THE HARD WORK YOU ALREADY DID.

Notes

_____

_____

_____

_____

_____

_____

_____

_____

_____

_____

ANITA KODDICK

IF YOU THINK YOU'RE TOO SMALL TO MAKE
A DIFFERENCE, YOU HAVEN'T BEEN IN BED
WITH A MOSQUITO.

Notes

_____

_____

_____

_____

_____

_____

_____

_____

_____

_____

VINCE LOMBARDI

THE SPIRIT, THE WILL TO WIN, AND THE WILL TO EXCEL ARE THE THINGS THAT ENDURE.

Notes

GUY KAWASAKI

YOU CAN BE RICH, YOU CAN BE POWERFUL AND YOU CAN BE FAMOUS, BUT YOU WON'T AMOUNT TO MUCH OF ANYTHING UNTIL YOU CHANGE THE WORLD.

Notes

_____

_____

_____

_____

_____

_____

_____

_____

_____

_____

GORDON BROWN

A BROKEN ECONOMY SHOULD NOT
MEAN BROKEN DREAMS.

Notes

_____

_____

_____

_____

_____

_____

_____

_____

_____

_____

CYRUS THE GREAT
(Founder of the Persian empire)

DIVERSITY IN COUNSEL, UNITY IN
COMMAND IS THE REASON FOR MY
SUCCESS.

Notes

_____

_____

_____

_____

_____

_____

_____

_____

_____

ALEXANDER THE GREAT

J.Chapman sc.

- THERE IS NOTHING IMPOSSIBLE TO HIM WHO WILL TRY.
- I AM NOT AFRAID OF AN ARMY OF LIONS LED BY A SHEEP; I AM AFRAID OF AN ARMY OF SHEEP LED BY A LION.

Notes

_____

_____

_____

_____

_____

_____

_____

_____

_____

_____

_____

SOURCES

The laws of thinking by E. Bernard Jordan
The power of positive thinking by Norman Vincent Peale
The secret of Loving by Josh McDowell
Secrets of the Journey by Mike Murdock
How to Get What You Want by Sidney Newton Bremer
This Life by Sidney Poitier
How to Make a Habit of Succeeding by Mack R. Douglas
www.olutosinogunkolade.blogspot.com
www.allgreatquotes.com
www.brainyquotes.com
www.thinkexist.com
www.wisdomonline.com

SOURCES